hooked through

hooked through

sara moore wagner

Five Oaks Press
FIVE-OAKS-PRESS.COM

Copyright ©2017 Sara Moore Wagner
All rights reserved. First print edition.

Five Oaks Press
Newburgh, NY 12550
five-oaks-press.com
editor@five-oaks-press.com

ISBN: 978-1-944355-25-8

Cover Art: Eric Moore
Cover Design: Stacey Balkun
Design inspired by Daphne Poulin-Stofer

Printed in the United States of America

Acknowledgments

Arsenic Lobster: "Coffin" and "Explaining Origins and Ending"

The Cincinnati Writers Project Anthology: A Few Good Words: "Like a Fish"

Illuminations: "Meleager"

Pacific Review : "A Mark on the World" and "I Imagine What That Story Was Like"

The Pittsburgh Poetry Review: "After the Burial"

Reservoir: "Try This Stillness"

The Wide Shore: "I Have No Love for Images"

The Yellow Medicine Review: "The Internal World of Objects," "Cattleheart," and "On Selfishness"

Contents

Like a Fish	7
Explaining Origins and Ending	11
The Internal World of Objects	12
On Selfishness	14
Try This Stillness	15
Cattleheart Complex or Rebirth	16
A Mark on the World	17
Reborn in the Body as Anne Askew	18
Coffin	19
As if Death Were Nothing	20
After the Burial	23
Meleager	24
I Want to Tell the Story of a Single Pumping Lung	25
Around an Opening	26
I Have No Love for Images	27
Until I Learn to Let It Go	28

For Cohen, my first born. I found these words for you.

Like a Fish

I.

Eleven Hours after he shot himself
I thought he was in pain because of the way
his mouth jerked like a fish on a line
until the water gathered on his skin
like dew.

The hole in his head, visible
because of the thrashing was
brown and ringed as the inside of a tree.

The nurse said yes,
that must hurt—his head—
he probably feels that.

Ringed round like the inside of a tree.

He hammered my mother's
wedding ring out of a quarter,
I say, because I don't know
what to look at. Too many
rings and hooks. Too many.

Death turns us all into fishes,
green and gasping.

II.

Later, I talk to my brother, he tells me we live
on a hill in the middle of the sky.

Look, all 'round is sky blue as the scales on a fish
he can't remember the name of. I say

it's ok.

No one remembers names.

We live in a house where our grandmother
 blacks the windows each night.

She does not black the windows
to keep out light, but to keep in darkness.

There are eyes out there
in the middle of the

sky, as gray now as a tarpon.
That is a fish, too. I think.

 I ask why everything must be related to water or sky.

My brother thinks they are the same,
reflections of each other.
But that is not true.

There is no water in sight—which is why he cannot really know
how blue any fish is but

there are hundreds of eyes in the windows.
Black them out.

III.

We are just
birds in an endless sky:
we carry worms in our beaks
like little severed tongues.

Father, my mouth is open,
hooked through.
Pull it out.

I.

"Inevitably they find their way into the forest. It is there that they lose and find themselves. It is there that they gain a sense of what is to be done. The forest is always large, immense, great and mysterious. No one ever gains power over the forest, but the forest possesses the power to change lives and alter destinies."

Jack D. Zipes, The Brothers Grimm: From Enchanted Forests to the Modern World

Explaining Origins and Ending

Five-hundred or forty years ago,
your heart was a small plum
in the paw of an animal no one ever named.
This creature had ears like cactus spikes,
and stone teeth. It was the ancestor
of your sensory organs.

Nothing is quite perfect
unless it is like this: half
eaten and unaware of what it does
or will do.

We are half-picked, rotting
fruit. Look at the way our lips still crack,
knees bend like emptying vines.

Our own tongues and teeth devour us.

The Internal World of Objects

There is a nest at the top of my spine
and, whether or not I like it,
a small squirrel climbs the staircase
of my ribcage and leaves things there—
some string, a french fry—
for the wood duck.

I say, wood duck, where do you come from?

This body is made of Ivory and silk, my nerves are
little exploding wires, he tells me:
Do not be afraid of the objects that make you.

But I run to the other animals, cowering
in chambers, the raccoon with its large eyes.

In his paw is a jug of my grandfather's best wine.
There is a door to fear, which I open.

I am afraid of what builds me. The little forest
of veins. If they pop—what pain.
I have violated the last rule.

And if I leave this place, as I am supposed to,
what quest will bring me back here?
Will he wait for me in the lake of my spilled blood?
Will he tell me to not be afraid of all
the objects he collects in me?

Will he paint a red feather on my forehead,
to mark me—

After—Wood duck, where is my wand or shoe
or harp? What can bring me back?

Out of my skin, a sturgeon gasps

in the air, floats over my fallen eyes.
I help him back in through the nose, pushing
his tattered scales deep into the cave of my skull.
He does not say thank you.

Second is a dead moth. I breathe onto
its dried body until there is something
moving, feed it to myself.

Third is a child, not mine. I say I don't know you
and put her into the palm of my open right hand.

They owe me something now.

When the wood duck comes to finish me, I think they will
save me.

At the end of this tale
I will get rich and marry a wood-cutter.
We will destroy this body.
We will build a home in a barren field.
I will sneeze out scales in the night:
feel the objects in my core rattle.

On Selfishness

Once upon a time, there was a girl
who thought this world would be better
looking if the people she loved were turned
into paper birds and suspended from the sky.

Her father was made of tissue and floating
just by the window, tired wings unraveling
slowly—a breeze could carry him out,
willy nilly.

There her grandfather was made of an old grocery bag,
his eyeless beak looming over her feet.

In her dreams he would swoop down
to gather bits of her toenails for his nest.
In the morning, she would wake to bloody sheets.

In the daylight, she watched
every single bird sway
gently with the vent aspirations,
too far apart to touch each other. Hers.

This room
is real
it lives
in the belly
of a swan.

One day that white belly will grow and hatch
like a blackbird pie—Oh—think
at how beautiful those birds and she
will seem to all of us.

Try This Stillness

You can be anything you want
to, a thimbleful of water, a single
sheet of paper, a doll on your
dead mother's shelf. If you want
to stay where something wants
you, be an object for once,
lie down. In fact, the other day
I was swimming in the over-
flowed river, my pockets full
of weeds, my hair so yellow it
could have been a patch of
sunlight and I thought
yes I am—what if we
are all like this, floating,
throats exposed like the smallest
stem. When I smash an insect
against my arm, there is a brown line
I don't wash. I notice the outline
of a wing. I notice my own bones,
how they move—I can be
something here, if I could just
kick my feet under and hold
on, plant myself
in a place where the meat
of me would not spoil. Then yes,
wait for the sun to dry me out, how
long would I stay there. Anything
you want to be, a picture
of yourself, even—a single
word. Anything.

Cattleheart Complex or Rebirth

In my childhood,
my cow stands in a field
with its white hairs and patches of brown
like a broken sky. Cow
with its brown eyes wet
and so full. It says, you

tell me what it means to have skin
and I will tell you what it feels
like to have wide eyes like an animal.

I found you standing
over the grave
of your mother and lowing.
This was after my father
cut off my hands. You told me
how to live in a world
as a beast would. When I speak now,
it is only lowing.

Stop—Let's imagine this pasture is an ocean.
The clouds are the same, no matter.

My cow bends down its knees
to see if there is a reflection
of this in the grass, but there isn't,
only the rocking of the world
and our solitary, wounded body.

I say, we are meat but it is so foreign
it could be the noise of a blue whale.

When we die, someone might
notice our grave and stare out
into the vastness.

A Mark on the World

When the doctor opens me up,
my bones are gold—
There is some enchantment in them.
The clock on the wall
rattles and speaks. Says,
put her as you found her,
into the womb of her mother.
When the doctor closes
my skin, my breasts
are two blinking eyes that watch
him move his needle back
and forth like a pendulum.
The bed quakes, the light
is a fiery god—Pantagruel
vomits up the sky.
I am a piece of tooth
in the great mouth of the world.
The dust of my core is
rot. Fix me,
oh you firmly planted
flower of the world.
These vibrating fingers
are my only stems.

Reborn in the Body as Anne Askew

I don't want to have to say again
what I mean by holiness. There is a brick
falling out of the side of your house,
I'm sure it will all fall apart before you
do something to fix it. God
damn this knocking on the inside of my rib-
cage. God damn the smell
of gunpowder. You know I am vile,
I'm ash. If I could speak a piece of bread,
and you'd eat it, it would be
a finger inside you sketching its
only wish on the lining of your stomach:
sowing.

I don't want there to be another
word or name for this quiet
in me. I want to blow my words
into a bubble, to feed them to you,
and then, to watch you pass them
as the land rejects a stone, slowly. Let
it tear you apart. And even then,
I will keep myself as I am now, and I will
say nothing has happened, I believe
you are making this up. You are,
actually—you are.

Coffin

Your breath
is a violent nest—children give their teeth
to the crow on your tongue.
When you open your mouth,

what are the eggs
you pull from your throat—
what sort of earth
births where it consumes—
as if we were conceived
from a piece of digested sky.

Even the tree outside—the dying leaves
on branches, gore.

I have a possum heart. It always
smells so sick. Watch it lay
like roadkill in my chest.

It is a gift for your cold eye,
orbiting my face like
a chunk of moon.

As if Death Were Nothing

In another life we greet ourselves in the mirror
as strangers, pull strands of hair and tiny insects
from between the threads of our clothing,
listen to the sound of the moon whisk
through the sky like a thrown pumpkin.

Trees look more like limbs,
like mothers. We are wolves at the root
of them, our bellies open and full of stones.

The pupils of our eyes are tiny bits of apple, as Eve.
Our mouths are full of milk. We tell our children
come outside for a drink, it is so dangerous
to stay indoors.

We take our heads into our paws
when it is time, lick the blood
of our last days until they seem like only reflection
and wind: sourceless, irrelevant light.

II.

"The word in language is half someone else's… it exists in other people's mouths, in other people's contexts, serving other people's intentions: it is from there that one must take the word, and make it one's own."

Mikhail Bakhtin, "Discourse in the Novel"

After the Burial

The skin on your hand is a web
in mine, a wisp of shadow.

Our hair is so golden—
under our eyes, the creases
look like tadpoles.

We walk down to the creek,
and I am stricken:
One day we'll catch our deaths

with cupped hands,
as we do the avalanche
of minnows—

your little fingers around a
wet rock, bent, already
hold an ending.

Meleager

There is so much fire under the floor here.
God help you if you walk barefoot
or your skin is made of dried leaves.
If your eyes are full of the particular fuel
that lights well on dry nights, like this one—
always turning.

This is the only light
after all. This night.

If you keep picking
grass even after there is no more fire
to light it with, when even the bones
of your house are fleshless,
your blood and your dry tongue puffed out
like a bird.

God help you when you think, this is what ash feels like.
A snuffed out brand. My mother, you kept me out
of the oven for so long, but still.
Not all life hinges
on fire or brands—
then, perhaps dryness keeps
it going.

I Want to Tell the Story of a Single Pumping Lung

My son says: what is air?
A long time ago it was a river. Before that
it was a snake. When your grandfather
pulled it out of the ground by its tail,
its fangs, yellow sharp suns, sunk into the soft
spot on his skull—soft because life was so much shorter then.

They say he prayed for a full week;
though, perhaps, his weeks were different from ours,
were concrete things like a half an inch of wear
on a stone. And maybe his prayers weren't prayers,
but birds that left his empty chest with fragments of bone

until it was all water, all around, even his body was that river.
And then, one day, something lighter,
like this thing we breathe in in in,
your teeth, tiny white bodies, floating.

Around an Opening

You'll remember,
before you were born
I did cartwheels over and over
on a row of graves
until my wrist snapped like the neck
of a bottle. So now,

forgive me that I am not better
at closing myself off,
even still.

Poured out
in this water, my nerves
resemble nets.
Oh child, magnify my true
skin. Make me a sinking
tapestry.

I Have No Love for Images

I've given up on the idea that a man
can crocus out of the earth all hair,
even his feet covered with hair, out of the earth
like a swollen root, his hands as soft and full
as berries. Because I am not
a tamer, but a shivering vine
and I also come
from this gorged stem, fruit
and not harvester. Forget
me for a second, you have given
up on this man out
of the ground because he is not
Adam but a fleshy bit of death,
and when he does get sick
and naked, when
he throws a bleeding thigh
so near the sun it hots
and smells like meat
your mother boiled down so low
it turned to dust. This thigh he cuts
from a living bull, from your sacred
body. And if you want to know,
I've been searching for him, too—
And I want to eat the stone bread
which stands for days, which stands for God,
to not sleep like a snake in a pile
of filth, to feed myself on air and the prettiest
slivers of sky. To be made
an equivalent beauty, or else
to not die is what I mean.

Until I Learn to Let It Go

I.

The foam on the lake is almost
the color of your smile—It's not you—
when I was a child, my brother
snapped back to cast
his fishing line and the hook
slipped into my palm like a gift,
worm and all. I remember watching
the struggle, the tug of the line,
the skin of my hand pull. You see
I am not used to letting go
or saying stop or anything
at all. I am a natural
triggerfish, ill-
tempered, marked by lines,
impossible, to catch, all spines
and teeth. Look at me here
on the beach—moving away,
transforming—unchanged.

II.

Death is nothing like
the stories I will keep
telling you, but neither
is life.

Notes

"The Internal World of Objects" follows Jack Zipes's eight functions of a fairy tale, from his article "The Changing Function of the Fairy Tale"

"Cattleheart" is the common name of the Parides butterfly

"A Mark on the World" and "Coffin" are related to Mikhail Bakhtin's idea of the classical and grotesque body in his work Rabelais and His World. In grotesque realism, a highly spiritual thing is degraded to the level of the body, showing they are all the same. Every part of humanity is made bodily. "Such a body, composed of fertile depths and procreative convexities is never clearly differentiated from the world but is transferred, merged, and fused with it"

"I Have No Love for Images" is based on the idea of Enkidu from the epic of Gilgamesh

www.ingramcontent.com/pod-product-compliance
Lightning Source LLC
Chambersburg PA
CBHW070104120526
44588CB00034B/2298